Social Smarts:
Manners for Today's Kids

by Elizabeth James *and* Carol Barkin

Illustrated by Martha Weston

Clarion Books/New York

Clarion Books
a Houghton Mifflin Company imprint
215 Park Avenue South, New York, NY 10003
Text copyright © 1996 by Elizabeth James and Carol Barkin
Illustrations copyright © 1996 by Martha Weston

The illustrations for this book were executed in felt-tip pen and ink wash.
The text was set in 13/17-point New Baskerville.

For information about this and other Houghton Mifflin trade and reference
books and multimedia products, visit The Bookstore at Houghton Mifflin
on the World Wide Web at (http://www.hmco.com/trade/).

Printed in the USA

Library of Congress Cataloging-in-Publication Data

James, Elizabeth.
Social smarts : modern manners for today's kids / by Elizabeth James and Carol
Barkin ; illustrated by Martha Weston.
p. cm.
Includes index.
Summary: Offers advice on how to handle all kinds of social situations and personal
interactions, presented with letters from two eighth graders to an etiquette advice
columnist, K. T. Answers.
ISBN 0-395-66585-X   PA ISBN 0-395-81312-3
1. Etiquette for children and teenagers—United States. [1. Etiquette. 2. Conduct of
life.] I. Barkin, Carol. II. Weston, Martha, ill. III. Title.
BJ1857.C5B34   1996
395'.122—dc20   95-35613
CIP
AC

BP 10 9 8 7 6 5 4 3 2 1

For our friends—your caring and consideration are the essence of good manners!

Alison, Amy, Andrea, April, Barbara, Bella, Beth, Betsy, Beverly, Boots, Brooke, Cagle, Carmela, Carol, Carolyn, Chris, Ciji, Debbie, Deborah, Deana, Denise, Diane, Dinah, Doreen, Dorothy, Edna, Elaine, Elda, Ellen, Elizabeth, Eloise, Elsa, Faith, Gail, Hannah, Helen, Jackie, Jamie, Jan, Jane, Janina, Jean, Jennifer, Joan, Joanna, Joanne, Jody, Joyce, Judy, Julie, Karen, Kathi, Kathie, Kathy, Kelsey, Kim, Laura, Lenore, Leslie, Lin, Linda, Lindsay, Lois, Lynda, Madlyn, Margaret, Marge, Marianne, Marilyn, Martha, Mary, Mindy, Nancy, Natalie, Nicky, Pam, Patty, Paula, Paulette, Pearl, Phyllis, Rosie, Ruth, Sandy, Sharon, Shirley, Stephanie, Sue, Susan, Suzy, Terry, Usha, Vicky, Wendy, Zay, Zoe

—E. J. and C. B.

To Ellen Blonder,
a dear friend
and the politest person I know.

—M. W.

Contents

A Few Words About Manners

WHAT DOES "GOOD MANNERS" MEAN? It's more than a list of dos and don'ts that you have to learn and follow so your parents won't yell at you. Good manners might be defined as a way of living that's based on the idea of the golden rule—treating others the way you would like to be treated yourself.

Millions of people live together on this planet, and each culture has its own definition of good manners—its own list of dos and don'ts. Another family's customs may seem strange to you. But the underlying purpose of every system of etiquette (or good manners) is the same: treating people with respect and consideration in order to make society run smoothly.

Remember when you were little and your parents kept telling you to "use the magic words"? Children learn to say *please, thank you,* and *I'm sorry* before they actually know what these words mean. When you use them now, you're aware of the idea behind them—acknowledging that other people have feelings and deserve respect.

This book is filled with practical information about manners in your everyday life, as well as tips and hints on how to deal with special problems. Advice from mythical columnist K. T. (Knows The) Answers offers specific solutions to frequently asked questions.

Good manners keep things orderly; when people know how they're supposed to behave and what to expect from others, they're less likely to feel embarrassed or out of place. Understanding the basics of manners gives you confidence in new or unfamiliar situations and makes it easy to figure out what to do.

P.S. If you have a question for K. T. Answers, here's where to send it:

> K. T. Answers
> P.O. Box 15801
> Beverly Hills, CA 90209-1801

Be sure to include your name and address so K.T. can send you an answer.

Chapter 1: Meeting People

Is this what happens when two of your friends who don't know each other meet at your house?

> **You**: *Oh, hi, Joe, come on in. We're just going to the video store.* (yelling) *Carla, are you ready?* (Carla comes in.) *Okay, let's go!*

Joe will probably figure out what Carla's first name is, but Carla won't know what to call Joe until you speak to him by name when she can hear you. And neither one of them will know the other's last name or what they might have in common besides being your friend. Wouldn't it make more sense to help them out?

You: *Oh, hi, Joe, come on in. My friend Carla is here.* (Carla comes in.) *Carla, this is Joe Rollins, my in-line skating buddy. Joe, this is Carla Stein. She and I both like horror movies, and we're going to rent one now. Want to come along?*

The whole point of making introductions is to make people feel comfortable and welcome, and, of course, to let them know each other's names. If you can add some helpful information, so much the better. Besides the person's name, you could say she's your math teacher or he's from Alabama or she has just won the school chess championship. This gives people who don't know each other something to start talking about.

Why do people think making introductions is so hard? The problem is that people know there is a rule about whose name to say first, and they're afraid they'll do it wrong. But introducing people is simple if you remember to do two things:

★Use both people's names twice ("Bob, this is Jim; Jim, this is Bob");

★ start with the more important person's name.

How do you know who's more important? It's a question of respect. Through the years, manners in our society have evolved to reflect respect for older people, women, and dignitaries or high-ranking officials. So in introductions:

★ Older people come before younger people;

★ women and girls come before men and boys;

★ VIPs come before less famous people.

How does that work in real life? When you're introducing your new friend to your grandfather, you say the older person's name first. Like this: "Grandpa, this is my friend Greta Green. Greta, this is my grandfather." It's polite to add your grandfather's name to the introduction so your friend knows what to call him; you could say, "Greta, this is my grandfather Mr. White." It might sound a little strange to you, but it's a big help to your friend.

You can see from this example that age counts more than gender. When introducing your teacher to your friend from out of town, you would say the teacher's name first because he's older: "Mr. Black, may I introduce my friend Sally Scarlet? Sally, this is my teacher Mr. Black."

How about introducing the boy who's just moved next door to your friend who's a girl? Since they're about the same age, you say her name first: "Vera, I'd like you to meet Greg Gray. Greg, this is my friend Vera Violet."

By now you've probably figured out that when the queen of England comes to your house, you'll want to address her first when you make the introductions: "Your Majesty, this is my father, Robert Brown. Dad, this is Her Majesty the Queen." Some people are considered so important that only their titles are used in introductions!

But don't worry if you start introducing people in the "wrong" order. Most people won't mind; they'll just be happy that you're taking the trouble to introduce them at all.

It can sometimes be a little tricky to know what to call an adult. Do you call your friend's mom *Sarah* or *Mrs. Silver* (or *Ms. Silver*)? It was easier in your grandparents' day when kids hardly ever called adults by their first names, but now it all depends on the particular situation. Generally speaking, you should use an adult's last name unless he or she has asked you not to ("Oh, Mike, you've lived next door since you were a baby—please call me Sarah").

But suppose you're with your friend Bob and you run into Sarah at the park? There's no reason to assume that she wants Bob to use her first name, so this is how you'd introduce them: "Sarah, this is my friend Bob Black; Bob, this is Ms. Silver, my next-door neighbor." If you're not sure what to call an adult, it's always safer to use his or her last name.

Divorces and remarriages can create even trickier problems in making introductions. You may feel very awkward spelling things out when you introduce your mother and stepfather to a new friend: "Mom and George, this is my friend Pam Pink; Pam, this is my mother and stepfather, Mrs. and Mr. Gold." But at least this tells your friend that while your last name is still Brown, your mother changed her name when she remarried. Now Pam won't embarrass herself by calling your mother Mrs. Brown.

What about introducing yourself to other people? Sometimes this is hard to do. You might feel shy in a group of people you don't know, and you may think you don't want to call attention to yourself in any way. But the people who don't know you may be feeling shy, too, and they probably can't think of a way to start talking to you. You'll be doing them, and yourself, a favor if you introduce yourself.

Take a deep breath and plunge in. Look at the person you're introducing yourself to and smile; stick out your hand to shake his or her hand; say, "Hi, I don't think we've met. I'm Richard Rose, Matthew's friend from camp." The other person will shake your hand and tell you his or her name, and then you can start chatting. You'll find that it's really not so scary—give it a try!

Are you wondering if there's a "right" way to shake hands? The answer is yes. In our society, a handshake is an established part of greeting a friend or a new acquaintance. Many people judge others by the way they shake hands. Giving someone a bone-crushing grip makes it look as if you're trying to show off your strength, while a feeble no-grip-at-all handshake gives the impression that you don't want to meet this person. A firm handclasp that doesn't go on too long is what you should aim for.

There are times when you don't want to, or can't, shake hands. But don't let the other person stand there with his hand out in midair—he'll feel like an idiot, and you'll seem quite unfriendly. Just explain the problem: "I'd like to shake hands, but my hands are covered with paint" or "I sprained my thumb" or "I've been holding a cold drink and my hands are freezing." The other person will understand.

Similarly, don't force a handshake on someone who may find it difficult to respond. A hand in a cast or an arm-load of groceries makes shaking hands quite awkward!

Sometimes you don't want to shake hands because you're embarrassed that your own hands are sweaty. This happens to a lot of kids and there's not much you can do about it. If you're wearing old clothes and can quickly wipe your palm on your pants leg, go ahead and do it. But if not, try not to worry. Your problem is more noticeable to you than to the other person. Most people have been through the same thing themselves and they'd rather have your smile and friendly hand-shake, sweaty or not.

What if you know you should introduce two people who haven't met each other, but you can't remember one of their names? In that situation, you have two choices. One is to introduce the person whose name you know to the one whose name you can't remember ("This is Tom Turquoise") and then pause; the other person is likely to introduce himself without your help. (By the way, that's what you should do if some-one is introducing you and obviously can't think of your name.) Your other choice is to smile at the per-son whose name you've forgotten and say something like, "Gosh, please forgive me, but I'm drawing a blank on your name—isn't that embarrassing?" Confessing this minor problem usually makes everyone smile.

If you're introducing someone to a whole group, it's better to say the new person's name ("This is Paula Pearl") and then let each of the group introduce him- or herself. Remembering a whole lot of new names all at once is hard; it's easier if each name is said by the person who owns it.

You may be thinking that all this introduction stuff is only for adults and that it doesn't have much to do with your life. But everyone appreciates the idea behind an introduction, which is to put people at ease in a situation that might be uncomfortable.

Dear K.T.:
I had a problem last week and I don't think

I handled it very well. On the first day of school, the principal called me into his office and introduced me to this new kid, Tom Tucker. Tom is in my class and the principal told me to show him around and help him out, since he didn't know where anything was.

I showed Tom a floor plan of the school. Then I took him to our classroom and introduced him to the teacher. Later, when it was time for gym, I showed him how to get there and I introduced him to a couple of my friends. But it was kind of hard to talk to him, because he didn't know any of the stuff my friends and I wanted to talk about, and he didn't tell us much except that he just moved here from Texas.

I don't think I did a very good job of introducing Tom to our school, but I'm not sure what I was supposed to do. Sign me,

Confused

Dear Confused:

It sounds to me as if you did pretty well, especially if you've never done this before. Some schools have hospitality committees to help new students, and you might suggest that your school get one going. As you discovered, it's not always easy to be responsible for introducing someone to a new place and a lot of new people.

You sound like a friendly person (that's probably why your principal picked you for the job) and it was a good idea to get Tom oriented with a floor plan and to introduce him to your homeroom and gym teachers and to some of your friends. But you don't mention lunch. It's easy for a newcomer to feel lonely in a cafeteria full of strangers. Did you invite Tom to eat lunch with you and your friends?

You say that it was hard to talk to Tom. Some people do have trouble joining in a conversation, but perhaps you and your friends were adding to the problem. Were you telling secrets or "in" jokes that he couldn't possibly understand without explanations from you? That can make a person feel excluded and unwelcome.

Often the best approach to a new person is to try to find out about his background and interests. This helps you carry on a conversation with him, since you'll probably find something you have in common, and it also means you can use those facts when you introduce him to others. To keep things from turning into a one-sided question-and-answer session, volunteer some information about yourself.

Remember that spending time helping a new person learn his way around doesn't mean you have to end up as best friends later on; it just means you're behaving in a kind, considerate way to someone who needs a bit of help.

Once you get going, it's not so hard to introduce a new person to your group of friends, your teachers, or whomever. But when you're the new person, it can be pretty overwhelming. You may feel awkward, and although you try hard to make interesting conversation, you may go away feeling sure you've made a fool of yourself. Try not to get discouraged; help is at hand.

Dear K.T.:

My dad got transferred and we've moved to a different part of the country. I miss my old friends and I haven't met anyone nice at my new school. It seems like no one even says hi to me, and I feel totally left out. What should I do?
Miserable

Dear Miz:

You have a difficult problem. It's very hard to move to a new place where you don't know anyone and where you have to start all over making a group of friends. Here are a few suggestions that will help you get started.

The most important thing is to take responsibility for the situation. Don't sit back and wait for other people to make the first move. After all, you're the new person, so it's up to you to reach out to them. Luckily, school provides lots of opportunities to do it.

Join some clubs, even if you're not sure you'll be interested. It's a great way to meet a few people at a time.

Accept all invitations—to parties, to study groups, to work on committees. You'll get to know a lot of different people this way.

Pick out a person in your class who seems friendly, and ask her or him for help—perhaps to show you how to use the library's computer system or where to get the best pizza in town. This contact will probably lead to a feeling of friendship that you can both build on.

Be friendly to everyone, even the kids you think are nerds at first glance. Appearances can be deceiving, and you may deprive yourself of a wonderful friendship if you don't give everyone a chance.

Finally, don't assume that the people you meet intend to be unfriendly. They may be so busy that they don't take time to get to know someone new. An extra step from you may be all that's needed.

Meeting new people can be both scary and exciting. That person you're introduced to at a party may change your life in wonderful ways, or may be so boring that you can't wait to get away (politely, of course). Whichever it is, you'll never know unless you keep yourself open to new people and new possibilities.

Introducing other people to one another will make the adults you know admire your courtesy and social skill; it will make other kids appreciate your generosity in making them feel comfortable. That's a pretty good payback for such a simple thing!

Chapter 2: At School

Whether it's big or small, your school is a public space that's shared by lots of people. Students and teachers, as well as a whole bunch of others, have to be there every day the school is open. When so many people are in the same place, there are bound to be some conflicts and stressful situations. But trying to be considerate of those you see frequently—your friends, the other students in your classes, your teachers, other school employees—pays off. Being considerate is contagious. The people you're nice to are likely to be nice to you. And maybe your group will start a trend and the whole school will be transformed!

Of course, most schools have actual rules—things like no running in the halls, no throwing food in the lunchroom, and no fighting. Many school rules are for the purpose of keeping people safe; no one wants two kids racing around a corner to crash into each other and have to go to the hospital.

Other rules are based on ordinary politeness. For example, keeping library books past their due date isn't just careless, it's selfish. When you've lost those books in the pile of laundry under your bed, you prevent other kids from using them.

You probably know that coming late to class gets you into trouble. That's because even when you try to arrive quietly, your slipping across the room and digging out your notebooks interrupts the teacher's plans for that class period. And of course, it also breaks the other students' concentration.

Whispering and passing notes in class is also rude and disruptive. It's true that not every class is totally fascinating, and when you're bored, making jokes with a friend can seem a lot more interesting than the lesson. This sometimes becomes the "in" thing to do in certain classes. But have you considered that besides being impolite, it can be destructive to you?

First of all, if you want to pass the course, it makes sense to pay attention in class so you know how to do the homework and pass the tests. Also, acting obnoxious probably isn't going to turn that boring teacher into an interesting one; it's more likely to make him or her worse. After all, why should a teacher bother to plan a terrific lesson if no one's going to pay attention? Finally, when you get so far behind that you need to go for extra help in that class, the teacher isn't likely to make a special effort for you. Don't imagine that teachers don't notice who's trying and who's goofing off.

The truth is, the teacher's job is to teach and your job is to learn, but the teacher is the one who's in charge. Since you don't have any choice about going to school, you might as well get as much out of it as you can.

Homework! It's a word that makes lots of kids groan. But it's not just a punishment that teachers think up to torture you. Homework has a purpose. It's intended to help you remember and understand what was taught in the classroom and to expand your knowledge of the subject. And look at it this way: it's fun to feel as if you know what you're doing in class, and doing your homework makes that possible.

Dear K.T.:

I don't know if my problem is serious or not. But it's bothering me. My social studies class this year is pretty hard, and every night for homework we have to read part of a chapter and answer some questions the teacher makes up. They're not fact questions, they're stuff we're supposed to think about, like "Why did the Egyptians have slaves?" It takes a lot of time, and the homework counts toward our grade.

Here's my problem. This girl in my class calls me almost every night to ask questions about the homework. She says something like "I don't get what Ms. Trask means in Question 1. What are we supposed to say?" She goes through the whole list of questions this way.

This girl is nice enough and I don't want to be unhelpful. But by the time we're finished, I feel like I've done her homework for her and she's using my work and my ideas.

Am I being selfish for not wanting to share my homework with her? What should I do? I'm feeling

Resentful

Dear Resentful:

You're definitely not being selfish, and I'm not surprised you feel resentful. Clearly, you're conscientious about doing a good job on your homework, and there's no need for you to do someone else's as well. The whole point of homework is for the student to learn something. You're not doing this girl a favor by letting her use your answers and avoid thinking things through for herself.

However, it may not be easy to stop her from calling you every night. You don't have to say you won't help her anymore. But you can tell her you can't talk to her that night on the phone. After this happens a few times, she'll probably get the message. If she persists, you might try saying that you'd like to help her but you don't have enough time. You might even suggest that she find a tutor to assist her—maybe your school has a tutoring program she could use.

Even though this girl has taken advantage of you, don't let the experience sour you on the whole idea. Giving and receiving help with homework is often beneficial to both people. But it works best when both of you participate equally, so one person isn't doing all the thinking.

When you have trouble with a subject, don't be shy

about asking for assistance. Remember, teachers are there to help you. They want you to succeed and to do well in their classes.

Find out when the teacher you need is available; then make an appointment, and show up on time. The clearer you can be about what it is you don't understand, the better. "I don't get what we did last week" isn't specific enough to let the teacher know what your problem is. It's a good idea to take notes so you'll remember the explanation and be able to refer to it later, if necessary. And be sure to say thanks for the extra time the teacher is spending with you.

Like any other part of life, school isn't perfect. A problem that comes up from time to time is cheating. Of course, everybody knows that cheating is wrong—even the students who are doing it know that. It's a kind of stealing, not much different from shoplifting or any other theft. A cheater steals your chance to succeed, and get a good grade, through honest work.

It can be a horrible shock to learn that someone you know has cheated.

Dear K.T.:

Something bad has happened, and I don't know what to do about it. We had a math test today in school, and afterward, two guys in the class were talking to each other about how they aced the test because they stole a copy of the answer sheet from the teacher's desk at lunchtime. I don't think they knew I heard them, and they acted like it was all a big joke.

I'm pretty mad, because what they did isn't fair to the rest of us in the class. If I tell the teacher what I heard, everyone will think I'm a tattletale and my life will be miserable. But if I don't, I'll feel like I'm letting them get away with something dishonest, and they'll probably do it again. What should I do? Sign me,

Upset

Dear Upset:

No wonder you're mad. It's very disappointing to find out that people you know have done something as rotten as cheating on a test. And it is often hard to know how to handle it. Many people would say that reporting their cheating to the teacher is the correct thing to do. But in real life, nobody likes a tattletale, even when he's right. On the other hand, doing nothing will keep you fuming and feeling that you've condoned their action.

However, there is another possible solution. Peer pressure is a powerful force in any school. Your opinion of these boys probably changed for the worse when you learned what they'd done, and I expect others would feel the same way. Why don't you tell a few of your friends about the cheating? Maybe a group of you will decide to tell these two that you don't think cheating is fair, and that next time it happens, you'll report it. Or you may find that the weight of other people's disapproval is enough to change their behavior.

Until you graduate, school is where you spend a large portion of your waking hours. Since so much of your life involves school and school activities, it's worth taking the trouble to make it something to look forward to. Treating others the way you'd like to be treated goes a long way toward reaching this goal.

Chapter 3: At the Table

WHEN PEOPLE TALK about good manners, they are often referring to table manners. Maybe this is because everyone has to eat, and meals bring people into close contact with others. When you're sitting next to or across from someone for the time it takes to eat a meal, you can't help noticing how that person behaves. If your brother grabs all the potato chips, you'll probably be annoyed at his selfishness; if your aunt spits some half-chewed meat into her plate as she laughs, you may feel both embarrassed for her and disgusted. And, of course, the other people at the table will notice the way *you* eat.

You probably know how you're supposed to act at the table; most people learn the basics of table manners from their own families. Rules like "Don't talk with your mouth full," "Keep your elbows off the table," and "Don't reach across the table for something—ask for it to be passed" are probably engraved in your brain by now. And it's not just your family that objects to certain behavior. Here's a list of the eating habits that a thousand people in a survey said turned them off the most:

★ making loud eating noises;
★ shoveling food;
★ licking a knife or eating food from it;
★ licking your fingers;
★ eating before others are served;
★ eating without offering food to others.

It's not always easy to follow all the rules of good table manners. For instance, not talking with your mouth full can be difficult, especially when you're at a friend's house and his mom asks you a question just as you've started to chew. What should you do? Try looking at her and raising your eyebrows to show you've heard her question; she'll realize right away what your problem is and will wait for you to finish.

Table manners are based mostly on consideration for other people and on safety. For instance, a good reason not to put too much food in your mouth at once is that if you do, you might choke on a piece of food that wasn't chewed well enough. That's a question of safety. On the other hand, a good reason to wait until everyone is served before starting to eat is to give the server a chance to eat his or her meal before having to serve seconds; that's based on consideration.

A meal is a social occasion, so most people try to make it a pleasant one. Instead of coming to the table all sweaty and grubby from the basketball court, take a moment to clean up. Try to leave your bad mood at the door and act as though you feel cheerful and friendly. Who knows, that pretense may turn into reality. To make sure the rest of your family doesn't waste away from starvation, take only your fair share of food. And remember to include everyone in the conversation so no one feels left out. If you keep these goals in mind, you'll be a terrific companion at mealtime.

Because a meal is a chance for family members to find out what's going on in everyone's life, it's polite to keep your attention on the conversation, and on the food. Reading, watching television, listening to your headphones, or talking on the phone during dinner makes it pretty clear that you're not interested in the people at the table. Of course, lots of families relax the rules and read newspapers at breakfast or watch a TV show together during dinner. Then they're sharing a meal in a different way.

In most families there is a difference between family manners and company manners. A meal you eat with just your family may be fairly informal. This doesn't mean it's okay to be rude or unpleasant; after all, shouldn't the people you love be treated with as much consideration as strangers? But when you have company, or when you're invited to a meal at someone else's home, it makes sense to pay a little more attention to the rules of politeness and take a little extra trouble. This shows your guests or your hosts that you care enough about them to behave courteously.

You may have heard the expression "FHB," which stands for "Family, hold back." When there are unexpected guests for dinner, these initials are supposed to be a secret code that tells family members not to take as much food as they normally would, just to make sure there's plenty for the guests. This expression is so well known that it's not much of a secret, but the idea behind it is the basis of "company manners"—making that extra effort to ensure that the guests feel welcome.

Of course, the specifics of table manners can vary quite a lot, depending on the type of food and the kind of meal it is. You can pick up french fries and burgers in your hands at a fast-food restaurant, but at a very fancy dinner party you're expected to eat almost everything with your silverware. (You're not likely to be served french fries and burgers at a fancy party, anyway!)

Paying attention to what's going on when you eat at another person's home is useful as well as polite. Part of your responsiblity as a guest is to fit in with your hosts' ways of doing things. If they pick up chicken pieces in their fingers to get every bit of meat off the bones, you can do the same thing; if they are using their knives and forks for the chicken, you should follow their lead. In the same way, if you wait for your hostess to pick up her fork before you dig in, you won't get caught by surprise when the others at the table bow their heads to say grace before starting to eat.

Watching your hosts and doing as they do is especially helpful when you eat with people whose cultural background is different from your own. Manners are not the same all over the world, although they are all based on the idea of consideration for others. For example, in Korea it's considered polite to slurp your soup and to belch at the table; this shows that you've enjoyed the food. In Germany it's impolite to put your hands in your lap during a meal; experts on manners say that in earlier times, not keeping your hands in view might have meant you were passing weapons under the table.

Nobody expects you to know all the variations in polite behavior among different cultures and ethnic groups. But staying alert and following your host's lead can keep you from feeling embarrassed in a new situation. This works at formal dinner parties and fancy restaurants, too. People sometimes say that table manners are just a question of knowing which fork to use; this is because formal table settings usually include three forks and perhaps three knives at each place. It can look a little intimidating, but you don't have to worry. The rule is, use the utensils that are farthest away from your plate for each course as it is served; when you're finished, leave the utensils on the plate to be cleared away.

At an elegant restaurant or a formal dinner (after a wedding, for example), you may be surprised to see a lot more plates and glasses at each place than you're used to. A very tiny plate is your butter plate (it may have a midget butter knife resting on it); a medium-size plate is for salad. Both of them will be to the left of your place setting. Your napkin will probably be folded on the empty plate at your place.

Two tips for fancy dining are:

★ Unfold your napkin and put it in your lap as soon as you sit down, and keep it there throughout the meal;

★ when the butter dish is passed, take some butter, put it on your butter plate, and spread it on each piece of roll as you get ready to eat it.

If you feel uncertain about which fork to use for the salad, or you don't know how to eat your artichoke or your snails, just watch how your host does it and do the same thing. If you feel comfortable with your hosts, you can admit with a smile that you're not sure how to go about eating the unfamiliar food and ask for advice. People are usually very happy to tell others how to do things.

What if you hate artichokes or you can't stand the idea of eating snails? Or what if you're allergic to one of the foods being served? This can be a little tricky. If the person who's serving the food asks if you want some of whatever it is, you can simply say, "No, thank you." You don't have to explain why you don't want it. But sometimes, especially at someone's house, people may insist that you try it; your hostess might say, "But it's my famous prune pie and everyone always loves it—just have a little." Pushing a person who has already politely said no is not very polite. But if it happens, you can just say, "No, thanks," again, or you can explain your reason for refusing. Keep in mind, though, that you don't owe anyone an explanation—a plain "No, thank you" is enough.

Sometimes your host serves you a little of everything, without asking what you want, and you end up with something on your plate that you really can't stand. This can happen at restaurants, too; the fried chicken you ordered might come with your least-favorite vegetable. Don't make a fuss about it—in fact, don't say anything. Just eat around it or push it to one side of the plate. When you're at someone else's house, you aren't required to eat anything you don't like, but you *are* required not to announce how much you hate it or ask for something different. This would hurt the host's feelings. And what if there's nothing else to offer you?

At any meal, it's polite to include everyone in the conversation, but it's especially important when there's a guest at your house. Telling family jokes without explaining them to the guest is a sure way to make him or her feel unwanted. And telling family secrets will embarrass your guest as well as the member of your family whose secret you're revealing. Ideal table conversation offers each guest a chance to talk about something that interests him or her; this generally leads to a discussion that includes everyone. It doesn't always work out quite this way, of course, but you can do your best to make sure each person gets a chance to talk and to listen.

Holiday dinners, when families gather for a special meal, are supposed to be lots of fun. But actually, these holiday gatherings are famous for causing tension and quarrels; you may see jokes about this in comic strips and on TV. Why should family get-togethers on holidays create so many problems? Maybe it's because relatives you don't see every day are both family and company at the same time, and sometimes those two roles don't blend very well.

Dear K.T.:

Yesterday was Thanksgiving, and I'm still steamed about something that happened at dinner. My parents invited about fifteen people, all relatives, so there was a pretty big crowd at the table. Halfway through dinner everyone was talking about other Thanksgivings in earlier years, and my uncle Greg looked at me and said, "Oh, I remember that Thanksgiving when Charlie was just a baby—he was the fattest thing I'd ever seen and there he was, rolling around on the rug in front of the fireplace in his birthday suit!"

Of course, everybody laughed like crazy, but I was really embarrassed. I couldn't think of anything to say, and I just wanted to run out of the room and not come back. It's not like it's the first time Uncle Greg ever told this story—he mentions it almost every time I see him, and I'm getting tired of it. But if I say anything about it, he says, "Aw, I'm just joking with you." Do you have any ideas on how I can make him quit embarrassing me with this baby story? If you answer, please change the names and sign me,

Embarrassed Baby

Dear E.B.:

Does it help at all to know that you're not

alone with this problem? Almost every family has at least one member whom everyone else finds embarrassing, rude, too loud, too sarcastic, or something similar. There's not much you can do about a person like that. He's probably been this way all his life, and at this point he's not going to change.

It seems to me that your uncle must be very fond of you—he's known you since you were a baby and he obviously has happy memories of that time. The problem is that he doesn't realize how much his comments embarrass you. Unfortunately, he sounds like a person who doesn't get embarrassed easily himself, and so he may never grasp just how painful you find his "joking" remarks. And you're in the tough position of being much younger than he is, which means you're supposed to be respectful. Remember, too, that although your uncle is "family," he's also a guest in your parents' house.

So what can you do to stop him? There are a couple of possibilities. If you can jump into the conversation when he's about to start recalling this incident, you might say, "Oh, that's the story about me on the rug in front of the fire. Don't you remember anything else about me when I was little, Uncle Greg?" If *you smile and say this in a pleasant tone, he shouldn't be offended, and maybe he'll realize that you, and the rest of the family, have heard the same thing too often.*

The other approach is to wait until he's finished and then say cheerfully to whoever is sitting next to you, "Uncle Greg loves to tell that story. I wish I could get Dad (or Mom, or Grandpa, or whoever) to tell some stories about when he was little."

Or you can just grin and bear it. Any of these methods is better for the sake of family peace than showing how embarrassed and angry you feel; making a scene will just upset everyone else and spoil the festivities, and will draw even more attention to the incident. If you can tolerate Uncle Greg with a smile, your other relatives are likely to sympathize with you and to think you're the one who's behaving like a grown-up. Maybe one of them will take him into a corner after dinner and suggest that he come up with some new stories for next year's Thanksgiving.

Even if you have pretty good table manners, things don't always go smoothly. This is bad enough when you're at home, but you feel even worse when you're out for dinner.

Dear K.T.:

I was invited for dinner at a friend's house and it seemed as if I did everything wrong. First of all, I was wearing jeans and a sweatshirt, and it turned out there were other guests and everyone was kind of dressed up and the table was set with a fancy tablecloth and good china. Then there was a plate of salad at everyone's place when we sat down, so I started to eat mine, and then I realized that no one else was eating theirs because the appetizer course was being served.

But the worst thing was that they had ice cream with chocolate sauce for dessert, and when I was pouring the sauce I spilled some on the tablecloth. I didn't even notice it right away, and I don't know if anyone else did. When I finally realized what had happened, I wasn't sure if I should try to scoop up the spilled sauce with my spoon, or tell my friend's mom about it right then, or wait until dinner was over, or what.

I ended up not saying anything until after dinner, and my friend's mom said not to worry, but I know it's her best tablecloth and my mom says chocolate is hard to wash out. I feel terrible about ruining the tablecloth and about acting like such a dumb klutz. Should I offer to buy a new tablecloth (I think it's a pretty expensive one)? I know my friend's parents will never invite me to dinner again!

Sally the Slob

Dear Sally:

It sounds as if you didn't have much fun at the dinner party, and that's a shame, because most of the problems weren't your fault. You certainly weren't to blame for being too casually dressed, since no one had told you dinner would be a fancy affair. You don't say whether your friend was dressed up. If she wasn't, you had no reason to feel uncomfortable; if she was, she should have offered to lend you something dressier to wear, or else assured you that it didn't matter in the least. As long as you looked clean and neat, I don't think you had anything to worry about, though I can understand your feeling a bit out of place.

As for the salad, you'll probably remember next time to watch your host and hostess for guidance about what to eat when; this will save you from embarrassment.

Obviously, the thing you're most upset about is the possibility that you've damaged an expensive tablecloth. When this happens, it's natural and appropriate to feel bad about it and to wish it hadn't happened. But do keep in

someone to dance? What if he/she refuses? What if you feel like a klutz on the dance floor? What if everyone else seems to be having a great time and you're not?

It sometimes helps if you remember that your friends probably feel insecure, too, no matter how self-confident they may act. Fear of not being popular, of not being accepted by the group, affects almost everyone. Try sharing your fears with a couple of friends. Saying "I hate these things; I feel like a total goof standing around the edge of the dance floor with nothing to do" will likely bring a sympathetic smile to your friend's face and a comment that starts with "Me, too." Fears that are shared tend to diminish in intensity once they are spoken aloud.

Focusing on someone else is another way to make yourself less nervous. Why not draw that timid new student into your conversation? Helping others cope with a difficult situation leaves you little time to worry about your own problems. You might even find yourself having fun!

Probably the most burning question in every girl's mind at these events is, how do I get that special guy to ask me to dance? It seems unfair that most girls don't feel comfortable asking guys to dance, but no matter how many advances there are in equality between the sexes, in many places it's still usually the guy's job to ask and the girl's job to wait to be asked.

Dear K.T.:

There's this really cute guy in my math class and we've sort of become friends. My school is having a dance next month and everyone goes. So I know he'll be there, but how do I get him to ask me to dance? I really want him to. One of my girlfriends said she'd be happy to go right up to him at the dance and tell him to ask me. Will this work? Please answer soon! I'm

Desperate

Dear Desperate:

I'm sure your friend means well, but I don't think this is a very good idea. Didn't you ever hear the story of Plymouth Colony's Miles Standish and his friend John Alden? Longfellow wrote a famous poem about it. Basically, Miles was too shy to ask the woman he loved to marry him, so his friend John asked her for him. Her reply is supposed to have been, "Why don't you speak for yourself, John?" Get the picture?

A much better solution would be to suggest to the school that some sort of mixer dances be included. Why don't they have a few "Ladies' Choice" dances? Or how about a "snowball," in which one couple starts dancing and when the music stops, they split up and choose new *partners? Folk or square dancing also gives lots of people a chance to dance together. All the other girls in your situation will be thrilled if you can provide a solution for their problem, too.*

But girls aren't the only ones who worry about dances. Boys look at things from another angle. They are usually the ones who have to walk across the floor feeling that everyone is watching their every move. It's not always easy for a boy to ask that special girl to dance. What if she says no? The fear of being rejected can keep guys huddled in the corner, unwilling to risk this embarrassment.

One way to make things easier for both sexes is to chat with one or two friends instead of seeking safety in numbers. It can be pretty hard for a boy to walk up to a big crowd of girls who are all busy talking to one another. And a girl who has decided to ask a boy to dance may be reluctant to approach a bunch of guys who are acting as if they wish they were somewhere else.

Another reason both girls and boys hang around on the sidelines at dances is that they're afraid they'll make fools of themselves on the dance floor. If this sounds like you, one solution is to take dancing lessons. Or try practicing at home with a friend. Or just go ahead and dance—most of the other people probably don't know what they're doing, either. At an informal dance, whole groups of people often start moving more or less in time to the music; this kind of group "dancing" makes it easy for anyone to join in.

One good thing about school dances is that everyone is invited. Not so with private events, whether you go with a date or not. Being invited does eliminate some of the fear of not being accepted. After all, you know you're wanted—this time. But what if you aren't invited?

It's obvious when you think about it that everyone can't be invited to everything. But that doesn't help much when you're the one who's left out. It's hard not to feel hurt and rejected.

Instead of sitting home feeling sorry for yourself, try taking some positive action. Maybe you and a friend can give your own party. Or find something else to do that night, like going bowling or to the movies. You might end up having more fun than you would have if you'd gone to the event, and you'll feel good about finding a way to cope with a problem that everyone experiences.

But what if you're invited to a date event—by the wrong person?

Dear K.T.:

I got into a fight with my mom about something and I want to know what you think.

A while ago, this girl I know invited me to her club's skating party. I'm not all that crazy about her—I mean, she's okay, but not the person I wanted to go with—so I said no. Then a few days later, a girl I really like invited me to the same party. But my mom said I couldn't go with the second girl after I'd turned down the first one.

The result was that I didn't go to something that I really wanted to go to. I think it was unfair of my mom to keep me from going—I know you'll agree with me. So I want to know what I can say to my mom in case this happens again. I don't want to have another fight with her. Please sign me,

The Peacemaker

Dear Peacemaker:

Sorry, but your mom was right.

Put yourself in the first girl's position. How

would you feel if someone who turned you down showed up at a party with someone else? Wouldn't your feelings be hurt? And don't think for a minute that she wouldn't figure out what happened. This kind of information always gets around.

The next time there's an event like this, you'd better go with the first girl who asks you or plan not to go at all—again. Going to a party with someone isn't exactly a lifetime commitment. You probably would have had fun if you'd gone with the first girl. She might easily have turned out to be nicer and more interesting than you thought. And just maybe the girl who called second would get the message to ask sooner next time.

Whatever social situation you find yourself in, it's always a good idea to try to see things from another person's point of view. Most kids have the same fears and insecurities. Anything you can do to make others feel included will be welcome. They'll feel better, and so will you. And this concern for other people could well reap you unexpected benefits.

Chapter 5: Parties

Parties are meant to be lots of fun, and usually they are. Whether you are giving the party or going as a guest, there are some common-sense ways of making sure the occasion is a happy one.

There are people whose full-time job is to plan and give parties. They know that thinking ahead is a key element in successful gatherings. So, while you may not want a career in party planning, it's still worthwhile taking some tips from the pros. Even a great party that seems to be thrown together at the last minute probably involved some skillful preparation.

As you wait for your guests to arrive, you'll look around and check that the pretzel bowls are filled and the sodas are ready to pour. But your obligations as the host don't end when the party starts. It's up to you to replenish the snacks if they run out—this isn't a guest's job. And it's also up to you to make sure all your guests feel welcome and included. If it's a small party and all the guests know and like one another, this isn't difficult. But if you had to invite your dorky cousin, do your best to introduce him to your friends and encourage them to talk to him. Remember, too, that it's not polite to hang out in a corner with your best friend for the whole party; part of your responsibility as the host is to mingle with all your guests and try to help everyone have a good time.

Usually there's a reason for every party, even if it's just "let's all get together." Whatever the occasion, if you're the host, you'll want to know how many people are coming so you'll have enough food to feed them. If you call to invite a few friends over, you'll probably find out right away who can come and who can't. But when you send written invitations, sometimes people don't get around to replying to them.

The letters *RSVP* stand for "Répondez, s'il vous plaît," the French words for "Reply, if you please." You'll see them at the bottom of many invitations, and they mean you are expected to tell the host whether you'll be attending the party or not. One hundred years ago, there was no need to write *RSVP* on an invitation, because no one would have dreamed of not replying. Today, many people include preprinted response cards, in already stamped return envelopes, with formal invitations to weddings or bar mitzvahs. They realize that if they don't do this, they'll never know how many guests will show up. However, just because some adults are rude and inconsiderate, you don't have to be; after all, it only takes a minute to respond. Besides, when you don't let someone know whether you're coming or not, you're letting him know you don't care much about his party.

When you give a party, sometimes you can't invite everyone you know. Your living room may not be big enough for fifty guests, or inviting everyone may be too expensive. So how do you choose?

If you're part of a group that does lots of things together, you can either invite the whole group or make the party much smaller and invite only your closest friends. But inviting every member of the group except one will guarantee hurt feelings.

When space isn't a problem, think about inviting people you don't usually hang around with but would like to get to know better. An invitation to a party is sort of an invitation to become friends, but without the commitment of spending a whole day or evening alone with someone you don't know well. Including a few new faces at your party will give your crowd a chance to broaden its horizons.

What if you have two friends who don't like each other? Go ahead and invite them both. But be sure to tell each of them that the other is invited. That way you won't be playing favorites, and the burden of whether to attend and be pleasant to the other person is on each of them. This works best in a fairly large gathering, not a pizza evening for four.

Dear K.T.:

My parents want to take me and some of my friends out to dinner and bowling for my birthday. The problem is that I'm good friends with eight guys but my dad said that five is the absolute maximum I can invite. I told him I would have trouble choosing who should come and he said, "Work it out."

How can I ask some of the guys to come and not invite others? I'm afraid the others will find out and they'll be upset. Maybe I could ask everyone not to mention it? Please sign me,

Hopeful

Dear Hopeful:

You're not just hopeful but downright naive if you think you can keep this party a secret. Even if your invited friends were careful not to mention it to the others, they'd certainly end up talking about it to one another. The uninvited are bound to hear about it, and their feelings will be hurt. Besides, if you and the friends you do invite form a conspiracy to keep the others in the dark, that's really not friendly!

If only five of your friends liked to bowl and the others didn't, you could use that as the basis for your decision and tell them all how you did it. But it sounds as though that simple solution won't work.

Have you considered asking your parents to change the party plans? Perhaps if they didn't treat everyone to dinner, they'd be willing to invite the whole group for bowling.

If this isn't possible, you might be happier spending your birthday with just one guest— whichever of these guys you consider your absolutely best friend. If it's only the two of you, the others will be far less likely to feel hurt and left out.

However, if you stick to your original plan, you should talk to the boys you don't invite. Tell each of them that you wish you could invite them all but your dad restricted the numbers. And say that you'll definitely invite them to something else—maybe you can plan to go to a movie together the next weekend.

Of course, that doesn't explain to them why they are the ones who didn't get invited. You have to hope that because they're your friends, they'll understand. They'll probably be faced with a similar problem someday.

Life isn't always fair or perfect, and that's especially

true when it comes to giving and receiving invitations to a party. All you can do is try to be as considerate of the feelings of others as possible. If you must exclude someone from the invitation list, see if the two of you can do something else together soon. If you can't accept an invitation, say why, and be honest. And if you just don't want to attend, make sure whatever excuse you used is the truth. That means you stay home and actually do that homework! Flaunting your lack of interest by going out that same evening will likely lose you a friend.

When you go to a party, you'll want to know if presents are expected. Nothing's worse than arriving at the door empty-handed and then seeing a huge pile of colorfully wrapped packages sitting on a table.

Congratulatory parties, such as those for birthdays and graduations, usually are gift-giving occasions. Even if you're told that gifts are not expected, ask around and see what the other guests are planning to do. If others have decided they're going to bring presents anyway, you may want to do the same. But gifts don't have to be superexpensive to be appreciated. If you're skilled at some craft, consider making a gift. A muffler knitted from inexpensive yarn that's the perfect color for your friend can end up being more treasured than an expensive piece of jewelry. You can even make a gift of your time by offering to take over your friend's dog-walking duties while she's away on vacation. At the party, give her a card with a handmade coupon tucked inside.

As the recipient, your job is to make every giftgiver feel valued, even if you're not totally thrilled with the present. Of course, you will thank the guests for their presents at the party. But it's also good manners to send thank-you notes afterward; it makes people feel that you really appreciated their thoughtfulness. (If composing thank-you notes is difficult for you, try writing them on picture postcards. They don't have room for lengthy messages.)

What if some people don't bring presents, while others do? The people who spent the time and money to get you something expect you to open the gifts so everyone can see them. But making a big deal about the presents you get may leave the guests who didn't bring anything feeling bad. There's not much you can do about this problem; go ahead and open your presents, but be sure to let all your guests know you're delighted they came to the party.

When you open gifts at the party, you may need to be a good actor. Usually friends know you well enough to give you things you want. However, there's often a clunker in the midst of all those wonderful presents. Pretend you love it. Always remember that it really is the thought that counts. You don't pick your friends based on what kinds of gifts they give you, do you?

Dear K.T.:
One of my friends gave me a birthday party

recently. It was lots of fun but when it came time to open the presents I felt kind of bad. A girl I know pretty well gave me a sweater that I hated on sight. I thanked her at the time and now I need to send her a thank-you note. But I don't know what to say. And I really don't want to wear this sweater. I'll be seeing her every day at school, so how do I explain why I'm not wearing her gift?

Perplexed

Dear Perplexed:

I've been in this same situation myself and I can understand how you feel—you don't want to hurt your friend's feelings, but you also aren't about to wear something you hate. It's not an easy problem to solve, but here's *one idea. You don't say whether you tried the sweater on at the party. If not, you can tell the giver that while it looked like the right size, it wasn't, and when you exchanged it, you had to take a different pattern or color. While I don't approve of lying, I also don't think it's kind to volunteer a hurtful truth.*

If you exchange the sweater now, you can say in your thank-you note that a sweater was just what you wanted, and that even though you had to exchange it, you'll think of her every time you wear the one you ended up with.

Sometimes a gift does come in the wrong size or in a fabric or scent you're allergic to. In that case, you are free to exchange it for something similar that you can use. A gift that you don't like but that can't reasonably be exchanged for something similar is one you're stuck with. Unless the giver has told you that you're free to return her gift for something you like better, and you're sure she means it, it isn't polite simply to trade the unwanted item for something else in the store. People usually go to a lot of trouble choosing the right present. If they wanted to give you a store gift certificate, they would have.

However, you aren't required to wear something you hate just because it was given to you. If the giver asks you why you don't wear it, you might explain that it doesn't look right with anything you now own and you're saving it until you buy something it will go with better.

The tact and delicacy required in dealing with unloved gifts is one reason many people end up giving things like books, CDs, or food. The food is presumably eaten and no one can reasonably ask why you're not reading the book he bought you or listening to that particular CD when he comes over to the house.

Parties that include adults can present different problems. Just about every kid attends a party like this at some point: a fancy wedding reception, a bar- or bas-mitzvah celebration, a confirmation or first communion party, or a graduation bash. No matter what the occasion, the adults are likely to be the hosts, and you will be either the honoree (the birthday girl, the bar-mitzvah boy) or a guest. In both cases you have certain obligations.

Some of these obligations are obvious. You can't act rude and boisterous; you can't grab all the best hors d'oeuvres; you can't leave in the middle of the speeches.

As a guest, you may find you don't know most of the adults at the party. It's not necessary to have lengthy chats with someone else's Aunt Alice, but you should be sure to talk with the hosts and thank them for inviting you. If the party is in your honor, the adult guests will probably be family and friends. It's important to talk with as many of them as you can, even if it's just to say, "Thank you for coming, it's good to see you."

Do you feel as if you never know what to say to adults in these situations? There's an easy way to solve this problem—just smile a lot and remember that the answer to most adults' questions and comments is usually "Yes," "Thanks," or "Fine."

"How's your little sister?" "Fine."

"Your parents must be so proud of you." "Yes" or "Thanks."

"You've grown so much!" "Yes" or just a smile.

You get the idea.

If your parents are divorced, these gatherings may create special problems. Naturally, both sides of your family want to celebrate with you, but they may feel they can't celebrate together. If you can, talk over your plans beforehand with both of your parents so any potential embarrassment can be avoided. Maybe both of your parents will attend your graduation from middle school, but only one will give you a party that day, and you'll go out to dinner with the other parent the night before. It's not your job to solve any problems they have with each other, but it will help if you're careful not to ignore either of them. When you make it clear that you want to celebrate your big day with both parents, they're likely to come up with a plan that works for everyone. After all, they're both proud and happy for you.

The whole purpose of giving or attending a party is to get together with your friends for some fun. Do the best you can in advance to sort out any possible problems. Then, when the party starts, forget the difficulties and have a good time!

Chapter 6: Difficult Times

Have you ever had to be in a hospital for a while? If so, you know how lonely and out of touch a patient can feel. Hospitals are busy places, full of so many routines that patients often complain they can't sleep because people wake them every five minutes to take their temperatures or give them tests. But all those people are strangers.

That's why it's important to visit a friend who is hospitalized for an operation or because of a serious illness. Your friend would no doubt love to see your familiar face instead of the constant stream of doctors, nurses, and technicians.

Before you set out for the hospital, there are a few things you need to know. Call first and make sure you're allowed to visit your friend; some hospitals don't permit visitors who are under a certain age, and visitors for very ill patients may be restricted to family members. If you can visit, ask what the hours are; some hospitals are fairly casual about visitors, and others have strict guidelines.

But no matter how lenient the hospital is, keep your visit short. Your friend will be thrilled that you showed up and may be unwilling to tell you when he's tired and it's time for you to leave. It's up to you to depart before he gets exhausted.

Hospitals can be scary places, and you may feel uncertain of how you should behave. Do your best to act normal, and try not to let the strange surroundings give you a fit of the giggles. If several of you are going together, don't let your enthusiasm turn into rowdiness. Even if your friend has a private room, boisterous behavior is inappropriate in a hospital. Remember to show consideration for your sick friend and for all the other patients as well.

It's not necessary to take a gift to a hospital patient, but you may decide you want to. Something cheerful and inexpensive is best. What about a funny card, a balloon or two, a jar of flowers from your garden, a small, lightweight game (playing cards or pencil-and-paper games are good), or a paperback book? Gifts of food are not a good idea; patients may have restricted diets, and there's usually nowhere to keep the food fresh.

If for some reason you can't visit a friend in the hospital, then be sure to write and call. Anyone shut up in a hospital for more than a day or two is likely to start feeling as though her friends have forgotten all about her. Your brief phone call telling her what happened in math class that day or how last night's basketball game went lets her know that she's not totally left out, even though she couldn't be there. And your cheerful get-well note or card is a reminder that you care about her and are looking forward to her return to school.

Should you ask your friend what's wrong with him? If he fell off his skateboard and broke his leg, he's probably happy to tell you all the gory details—but he's probably already on his way home. Doctors try not to keep people in the hospital even overnight unless they are seriously ill or badly injured. So your friend who is hospitalized may find it too sad or too difficult to talk about his medical problem. Be sympathetic and let your friend know you're there if he wants to talk, but don't push him; he'll share his thoughts and fears when he's ready.

If someone you know is going to be in the hospital or recovering at home for more than a few days, one way you can make yourself especially valuable is to take along homework assignments when you go to visit. Helping your friend keep up with what's happened in class will be good for you, too. There's no better way to make sure you understand something yourself than to try to explain it to another person.

Another way you can be helpful to your friend and her family and have a good time yourself is to offer to "babysit" with your friend some afternoon or evening once she's back home. This way you and your friend can spend time together and her family can get a break from taking care of her. Just keep in mind that someone recovering from a serious illness or surgery needs to take it easy. Be sure sickroom activities don't become so stimulating that your friend suffers a relapse!

Once your friend gets better and goes back to school, she may want to prove to herself and everyone else that she's totally back to normal. This is certainly understandable. After all, she's missed a lot while she was gone and she wants to catch up on everything all at once. You can't tell her what or what not to do, but you don't need to encourage overexertion. Instead of planning an entire day at the mall, why not make your first trip short and restful—maybe lunch and a movie?

Even more difficult than a friend's illness is when a friend's relative dies. What are you supposed to do then? Many people are so concerned that they won't say or do the correct thing, they end up not doing or saying anything at all. But some sort of acknowledgment of the death is essential, even if you feel a little awkward making it.

When someone dies, most people realize that there's no way to change this sad fact. While somewhere in their hearts they probably wish they could reverse time and make that friend or relative alive and well again, they know this isn't going to happen. What they want now is to feel that the person who died made some sort of difference in the world and will remain alive in other people's memories. They want to know that others remember that person and recall how kind or funny or smart or good he or she was.

If you keep this in mind, you'll see why it's important to write a note or make a phone call after a death. And you don't have to have known the person who died personally to understand how sad the death is for your friend.

Dear K.T.:

I have a problem and I need help fast. I just found out my best friend's grandfather died. My friend—I'll call him Jeff—seems pretty upset, even though his grandfather was very old and in a nursing home. Jeff is a really good buddy and I don't want him to be sad. He told me when the funeral's going to be and I got the feeling that he wanted me to go. But I never even met Jeff's grandfather. Besides, I don't know how to act or what to say at a funeral. What do you think I should do?

Ignoramus

Dear (You're Not an) Ignoramus:
Don't put yourself down for not knowing

how to behave at a funeral. Many people feel intimidated when they attend one. All you need to remember is to act respectful and do things the way everyone else does. Since different religions have various customs for funerals, it's impossible to know in advance exactly what will happen. But you'll be fine if you watch what the other people are doing and follow their lead.

It sounds as though Jeff really needs your friendship right now. If you possibly can, I'd suggest you go to the funeral and be there to support your buddy. His parents may be so upset themselves that they haven't given much thought to Jeff's grief, but even if they have, Jeff can use someone his own age to help him through this sad time.

It doesn't matter that you didn't know his grandfather. Jeff is the one who needs your comfort. Also, don't worry about what to say before or after the funeral. Something simple like, "I'm sorry your grandfather died; I know he was very special to you," is perfectly fine. Try getting Jeff to talk about some of the good times he had with his grandfather. If you remember any stories Jeff told you about the two of them, be sure to mention them.

Many people don't handle news of a death well. They feel uncomfortable about it and so *they try to pretend that nothing happened. But that isn't very helpful to the grief-stricken survivors. By encouraging Jeff to talk about his grandfather, you help him keep these important memories alive. This is one way you can be a good friend.*

Most people know enough to send sympathy notes when someone dies. But how are you supposed to act when your friend's relative is terminally ill?

Dear K.T.:

My friend "Alice" has a serious problem and I don't know what to do. I think Alice's mom is dying of cancer. Alice hasn't exactly told me, but my mom says it's true. Nobody seems to know how long she has to live. They just keep taking her to the hospital and bringing her home, but I know they've stopped the chemotherapy because it wasn't doing any good.

I can't figure out if it's better for me to talk to Alice about this or not. Part of me feels that if she wanted to tell me about it, she would have. But she acts so different now and I wish I could find a way to help her.

Sad for My Friend

Dear Sad:

What a tragic story; no wonder you're sad

for your friend. You don't say how big Alice's family is—if she has brothers or sisters—and how her father is handling this terrible situation, but I would guess that Alice needs to talk and just doesn't know how to begin. You might try asking how her mom is doing when the two of you are by yourselves—for instance, taking a walk together. But if she doesn't give you much of a response, don't press her for information. She may be afraid that by putting her fears into words, she'll make them come true.

The best way you can help Alice is by continuing to be her friend. Include her in all the activities you usually do together and counsel your mutual friends to act as normally as

possible. Whispering about Alice or her mom or cutting a conversation short when she comes into a room will only make your friend feel more alone and left out than she does already.

You don't mention this, but I wouldn't be surprised to learn that Alice is going through some pretty severe mood swings. If so, try to ignore her occasional bad temper and don't get dragged into foolish arguments with her. Children often feel responsible for their parents' poor health or death, and Alice may want to start a fight just to prove to herself that she's really as rotten as she fears she is.

My heart goes out to you and your friend. Even the best doctors in the world can't predict how long a very sick person will survive, so this could go on for quite a while or be over fairly quickly. But, no matter how sick her mom is, don't be deluded into thinking that it will be better for Alice when her mother dies. What she probably wants most in the world is for her mom to be well and healthy again. That's what people mean when they say, "Where there's life, there's hope."

I'm sure you'll be there with a hug and a shoulder to cry on when Alice's mother finally does die. In the meantime, be kind to yourself as well. It sounds as though you're trying to be *the best friend anyone can be, but recognize that this is a very difficult time for you, too. Good luck.*

Sickness and death are a part of life, and ignoring them won't make them go away. But although you can't prevent them from happening, that doesn't mean you can't help. The three key words to remember are *write, call,* and *visit*. Write a condolence note to your friend who's lost a loved one; send get-well cards and notes to friends who are sick or injured. Call to cheer your sick friend and keep him from feeling left out; keep in touch with your bereaved friend to let her know that your friendship is still there for her as she deals with her grief. If visits are allowed for your friend who's shut in with illness or surgery, go as often as you can. You bring with you the outside world that he's missing while he's in bed. Your appearance at a funeral or your visits to your bereaved friend's house are extremely comforting. You don't need to say much, but your very presence can give her strength and courage.

Chapter 7: On the Phone

TALKING ON THE TELEPHONE is about as basic as breathing—it's hard to imagine life without it. For most people, it's the main method of communicating with those they aren't looking at face-to-face. Every day you have lots of chances to judge how people use the telephone—rudely, helpfully, demandingly, or whatever. The people at the other end are judging you, too. Luckily, it's easy to make a good impression on the phone.

When you make a phone call, it's polite to identify yourself as soon as someone answers. People don't enjoy being embarrassed when you say "Guess who this is?" or "Hi, it's me!" and they don't recognize your voice. And you'll win points with your friends' parents if you start out with "Hi, this is Kim Kraft. May I talk to Linda?"

Speaking clearly is especially important on the phone, because the other person can't see you. He or she can't look at your face or your gestures to get clues about what you might be saying.

Before you pick up the phone, look at your watch. Is this a good time to call your best friend? Or is he likely to be eating dinner or asleep? Most people don't like to be interrupted at meals, except in emergencies. And late at night, even if you're sure your friend is still up, other members of his family may not be.

Dear K.T.:
My friend, I'll call him "Joey," has a habit of calling me kind of late at night. He's a real night owl and I'm usually up when he calls, so it's no problem for me.

But last night when Joey called near midnight, my dad got so angry that he made me get right off the phone. I didn't even get a chance to hear what Joey was going to tell me. And it was important—I needed to know that his mom couldn't give me a ride this morning to school.

I don't see why my folks care what time I get my phone calls. I always pick up the phone on the first or second ring. How can I get them to ease up?

Frustrated

Dear Frustrated:

I'm afraid that you aren't going to be happy with my response to your problem. I don't know how you can get your parents to ease up—in fact, I agree with them completely. There's nothing more annoying, and sometimes frightening, than hearing the phone ring late at night. Even if they aren't startled out of a sound sleep, many adults assume that a late-night call means an emergency.

You don't say so, but I expect your parents have already made their feelings about the timing of Joey's calls clear. Have you told Joey not to call you at that hour? If not, why not? Your friend's behavior when it intrudes on your family is your responsibility. I'm sure if you explain to him how upsetting these calls are to your parents, he'll find a way to call you earlier.

By the way, I hope you don't call anyone this late!

No matter what time of day or night it happens, a call to a wrong number is annoying. When you reach a wrong number, don't just hang up without saying anything. For one thing, it's rude; you've made someone answer a call that isn't for him or her. But more important, you need to find out what the problem is. Did your fingers slip as you hit the buttons, or do you have the number written down wrong? The way to find out is to say to the unfamiliar voice, "I'm sorry, I must have a wrong number. Is this 555-1234?" The answer will tell you where you made your mistake. Apologize again before you hang up, and be careful next time you try to place the call.

When you answer your phone and someone asks you to send a taxi to Maple Street, don't just say, "Wrong number," and hang up. You're likely to get another call from the same person in a minute or two. Instead, ask, "What number are you calling?" If it's not your number, you can tell the person she has misdialed; if it is your number, tell her she's dialed correctly, but this isn't the taxi service. Then she can check the phone book before she tries again.

Often people who call wrong numbers ask who you are or what number they've reached. These are inappropriate questions that you shouldn't answer. Giving out your name or phone number to strangers is never wise.

Families have different ideas about the way phone calls should be answered. Some prefer that you say, "Jones residence," while others like a simple "Hello." Do it the way your parents want it done; if you answer the phone at a friend's house, follow that family's custom. (If you need to make a phone call from someone else's house, keep it short, and offer to pay for toll charges.)

When you answer a phone call that's for someone else in your family, the polite thing is to say, "Hold on a moment, please," and then go and find that person. Clattering the phone down on the table and yelling, "Robin, it's for you!" is painful to the caller's ears. Remember, too, that even things you say in a normal tone can be heard at the other end of the phone. Don't make personal comments about the person who has called. Saying "JoAnn, it's that idiot Wilma again" will embarrass your sister and hurt Wilma's feelings; this thoughtless behavior makes you look stupid.

When the call is for someone who isn't home, it's important to ask if you can take a message—and then to write it down! You may think you'll remember to tell your dad that the plumber can't come tomorrow after all, but it's awfully easy to forget. Most families try to keep paper and pencil near the phone. If they aren't handy, ask the person to hold on while you get them. People are usually happy to wait in the hope that their messages will be passed on correctly. And if you're not sure how to spell the person's name, don't hesitate to ask.

Have you ever listened to a message on your answering machine and been frustrated because you couldn't understand it? Perhaps the person spoke so softly you could only hear a faint mumble, or perhaps she just said, "Hi, it's me, call me back." You were left wondering who it was and when and why she called. How can you avoid doing this yourself when you leave a message on a machine? Be prepared! Always give your name and phone number—your best friend no doubt knows your number by heart, but if he's been rushed to the hospital, you'll want his mom to be able to call and tell you. It's also smart to say the time and date (or day of the week) of your call. People don't always clear their messages right away, and it's helpful for your friend to know he's talked to you since your call and he doesn't have to call you again.

Most families have one answering machine that everyone shares. This means it's easy for messages to be accidentally erased, or to be kept for days even when they're no longer needed. It's a good idea to talk this problem over with your family and make a plan. A couple of possibilities are to keep all messages on the tape until the next morning, or to write down the information and erase them as you go.

But what if your family has carefully saved a message for you that you'd rather not get?

Dear K.T.:
    I have a problem I don't know how to solve.

A girl I know at school likes to spread mean stories about other kids. She can be pretty funny sometimes, and I have to admit I've laughed at some of her nasty imitations. But I guess that made her think I wanted to hear her gossip all the time. Now she calls me on the phone almost every day. Luckily, a lot of times when she calls, I'm not home. But here's my question: when she leaves a message for me, do I have to call her back? I think it's rude when people don't return my calls, but I really don't want to talk to this girl.

Turned Off

Dear T.O.:

The short answer to your question is no—you don't have to return a phone call if you don't want to. A telephone call is as much of an intrusion into your home as a person who comes to the door and wants to be let in. In both cases, you get to decide if you want to keep that person out. But be aware that your decision will have consequences, and you should be prepared to accept them.

Your problem is one that existed long before telephones did. When people made formal calls at the homes of their friends and acquaintances, the butler or the footman told them that the lady of the house was "at home" or "not at home." This didn't necessarily mean she was or was not in the house at the time; it simply meant she did or did not want to see the caller.

Obviously, if the caller knew the lady was there but the butler said she was not at home, the caller might feel insulted. This was a risk the lady had decided to take. Similarly, if you never call this girl back, she may feel hurt or angry.

Probably she will also ask you why you didn't return her call. It's not okay to lie and say you didn't get the message, which is likely to prolong the problem anyway. But you don't have to tell her you can't stand listening to her unpleasant remarks. You can say something polite but vague, such as "It wasn't convenient" or "I was busy with a lot of other things." Both of these are probably true in some sense. If you continue this tactic, she will give up after a while and stop calling you.

You've already figured out that laughing at her stories encouraged her to tell you more of them. Let's hope that your not participating in her meanness will have the opposite effect and she'll stop passing on her nasty tales to you.

Sharing a family phone requires the same kind of consideration as any other social activity. This is hard to remember sometimes, especially when you're engrossed in a serious discussion or an exchange of secrets with your best friend. But kids monopolizing the phone is probably the biggest complaint parents have.

Of course you understand that when your parents need to use the phone, or when they're expecting an important call, you have to leave the phone line free. But if no one else is using it, why can't you keep talking?

That question may not have an answer that will sound reasonable to you. However, it makes most parents crazy when their kids are on the phone for hours at a time. This is a fact of life. If your phone has Call Waiting, that helps; at least family members know they're not missing incoming calls. But it doesn't change the fact that many parents think their kids should have something better to do than talk on the phone all day.

Why not ask your parents what time of day would be best (and least irritating to them) for your long calls? You might promise to keep most of your calls short and save any lengthy ones for the time periods you all agree on. Your parents will be pleased that you're trying to understand their feelings and to come up with a solution that makes everyone happier.

Your friends' families may have rules about long phone calls, too. If you think you're going to talk forever, ask right away whether you're calling at a good time. This will reduce phone friction at your friend's house as well as yours.

When someone calls you at an inconvenient time, like the middle of dinner, explain why you can't talk then, and arrange to return the call some other time. There's no need to be impolite to the friend who's calling, but you don't want to be rude to your family either. Chatting on the phone during a meal makes it clear that you think the call is more important than spending this time with your family.

Now that lots of people have Call Waiting, your phone conversations are likely to be interrupted. The person you're talking to may not hear a click when the other call comes in on your phone, so be sure to explain why you're disconnecting for a moment. Saying something like "Do you mind holding on a moment? I've got another call" makes things clear.

When you say it will be only "a moment," stick to it. It's easy to get drawn into conversation with the second caller, but the first one will be understandably annoyed at being abandoned in the middle of a chat. If it's urgent for you to talk to the second caller right away, take time to be polite; put the second person on hold while you explain the situation to the first one and tell him you'll call him back later. This kind of thoughtfulness is always appreciated.

That pencil and paper by the phone is very important when you have Call Waiting. Jot down the name, and phone number if necessary, of the second caller. Otherwise, you're very likely to forget who it was by the time you finish your first call.

When you're on the phone, remember that background sounds carry across the line to the person you're talking to. Although you can hear over the blasting music in your room, your friend may not be able to understand what you're saying. Even softer sounds can be annoying—other people talking in the room, clattering dishes, running water, and so on. You've probably noticed that if someone is crunching celery or eating an apple while talking to you, it's very hard to hear. Besides, it's just as rude as talking with your mouth full at the table. If you get caught with a bite in your mouth, finish chewing quickly, apologize, and don't eat more till you're off the phone.

Most people want their phone conversations to be private. You probably wait until your sister hangs up the other extension before you start chatting to a friend. Respect other people's privacy—don't let yourself be tempted to eavesdrop.

However, some kinds of phone communication are not as private as you might think. For example, e-mail and cellular phone calls, which are supposed to be personal messages, can be tapped into by other people. If you use a fax machine, anyone at the receiving end can see what's transmitted. So you may want to keep your extraprivate discussions for the regular telephone.

The phone has become a vital part of our daily lives, especially in an emergency. Calling 911 is the quickest way to get help from police and fire departments and emergency medical services. If you ever need to call 911, try to stay as calm as possible. Speak clearly, give your name and address, and say what the problem is. Don't hang up until the emergency operator tells you to. If you dial 911 by mistake, do not just hang up; explain that your call was an error, so the operator won't have to trace the call to make sure everything is okay.

Other kinds of help are available by phone. Look in the front of your phone book for the numbers of various crisis lines, such as suicide prevention and help for families of alcoholics. The people who answer these phone lines won't ask your name; they are sympathetic listeners who can offer lots of good advice.

Telephones are sometimes used in ways that are annoying or even frightening. If you've ever received an obscene phone call, you know how scary they are. People who make such calls are warped, and they get satisfaction from hearing your response. The best thing to do is to hang up quietly as soon as you realize what kind of call it is. Be sure to tell your parents so they can notify the phone company.

If you are home alone, you may not feel comfortable saying so to a telephone caller. Talk over with your parents the best way to handle this situation. It doesn't always work very well to say something specific, such as that your mom is in the shower; when she doesn't call back in a few minutes, the caller is likely to figure out that you weren't telling the truth. Try to come up with a standard reply you can use that won't sound obviously untrue. Many people say, "She's unavailable right now," which is both true and vague enough about the length of time it may take her to return the call. If the caller persists and asks when your mom will be available, just say, "I'm not sure, but I'll tell her you called."

Telephone pranks or "joke" calls are extremely irritating to anyone who receives them. If you and your friends think making such calls might be funny, stop and consider; you'll be intruding on other people's lives, making them drop what they're doing and answer the phone for no good reason, and they won't find it cute or amusing.

A little good sense and common courtesy can make using the telephone pleasant and problem-free, for you and for the people you talk to. And that's the whole idea.

Chapter 8: In Public

Have you ever felt discriminated against simply because you aren't an adult? Maybe when you and your friends are wandering through the local mall one Saturday afternoon, you notice that salespeople seem to avoid you whenever you walk into a store. *What's the matter with these people?*, you ask yourself. After all, your money is as good as anyone else's.

It's no fun to have people look at you as if you're from another planet. And it isn't fair. However, many adults who deal with the public, such as sales clerks, theater managers, bus drivers, and restaurant workers, look at a group of kids with something approaching fear. They may have had bad experiences with kids who are loud or rude or otherwise obnoxious. If the store clerk keeps an eagle eye on you, he may have been ripped off by young people who were shoplifting. Now he's suspicious of every kid who walks into the store.

It isn't possible to change the world overnight, but you can try to change the way people treat you in public places. How? By thinking about how your behavior looks to them, and by treating them the way you'd like to be treated. Try pretending that the adults you're sharing space with are your favorite aunt and uncle, people whose opinion you care about.

You may not realize how loud you and your friends sound, especially to adults. It's easy to get carried away by a joke that one of the group tells as you're all waiting in line to buy movie tickets. Before you know it, all of you are screaming and laughing your heads off. That kind of joviality easily gets out of hand. Bear in mind that the people around you didn't hear the joke (even if they did, they probably didn't get it). They may be happy to see you having a good time, but it won't be fun for them if they can't have their own conversations because you guys are so loud. And if laughing escalates into shoving and pushing, no one is going to appreciate sharing space with you.

Okay, you may be saying to yourself, that kind of behavior is obnoxious. But what can you do about it?

Dear K.T.:
This may sound like a dumb problem to you and I'm not even sure why I'm writing

you about it. But the other night, three of us went to a movie, and my buddies kept on goofing off and talking to each other after it started.

I could hardly hear what was on the screen myself and I was embarrassed because I could tell that the people around us were getting kind of mad.

I didn't know what to do. I mean, I don't want to come off like I'm the teacher or something. But I was worried someone would report us to the manager and we'd get kicked out. After a while, the guys finally quieted down, but the movie was pretty much ruined for me by then.

What should I do if this happens again? Please don't use my real name; I don't want my friends to think I'm some sort of a

Goody-goody

Dear Goody:

Your problem is not uncommon, for kids and adults alike. Good for you for trying to find a solution. Lots of people don't look for help with a difficult situation but just sit around nervously hoping it won't happen again.

First of all, I wonder why your friends paid to see the movie if they didn't want to watch it. But I'll bet you sometimes wonder the same thing!

It sounds to me as though you were as much annoyed with your friends as you were embarrassed by them. They put you in a tough spot with their rude behavior. You don't say whether you asked them to keep quiet so you could hear the movie. That's certainly the first thing to do, and you don't have to make a big deal about it. A simple "Keep it down, guys, I can't hear" might be enough.

Another way to handle the problem is for you to get up quietly and move to another seat a few rows away. That way you'll be able to enjoy the movie, and you'll also let the people around you know that you don't appreciate your friends' behavior. Then, if anyone gets kicked out for making too much noise, it won't be you.

But I wonder if going to a movie with these two guys is a good idea to begin with. They must have some sterling qualities or they wouldn't be your friends. Maybe being in a movie theater just brings out the worst in them. Why not find someone else to see movies with and save your time with these two friends for situations where they act like regular people?

What if you were a complete stranger watching how you and your friends behave at the mall or in some other public place? Would it look as if your group thought there was no one else on the planet? Sometimes when you're with a bunch of friends, you have so much fun together that you completely ignore everything, and everyone, else. Maybe you and a pal love to zoom down the sidewalk on your skateboards, and you don't even notice that the pedestrians have to jump out of your way to avoid being run over. You may feel you're in total control, but others are likely to view your actions as a threat to their safety. Can you blame them for being annoyed?

Boom boxes are another source of irritation to lots of adults. You've no doubt heard a million times that music played at high volume can damage your hearing. Even if you think you don't care about that, the other people who have to listen to your tape or CD do—and besides, they probably don't like your taste in music! Inflicting loud noise of any kind on innocent strangers who are minding their own business is a sure way to make yourself disliked. Then, when you ask the man standing at the bus stop if he can change a dollar for you, he won't even check his pockets before he says no. So why not get a set of headphones, and use them?

You may wonder why the sales clerks shudder when you and a couple of friends wander into the shop. Here's one possible reason. Maybe the last three groups of kids spent hours trying on zillions of items in different colors and sizes, made the other customers wait for dressing room space, left all the clothes on the floor of the dressing room, and then walked out without buying a thing. After they were gone, the sales clerks had fun picking up all the clothes, brushing off the dirt, and hanging everything up again on the correct racks. Later, they found out from other customers that several of the items had makeup smears and ripped seams.

Of course, you can try on as many clothes as you like in a store, and you aren't required to buy anything. But if your Saturday afternoon activity is "shopping" of this kind, at least take the trouble to keep the clothes clean and neat, and let a possible paying customer have a turn in the dressing room.

Being aware of the other people around you can make you see your actions in a new light. For instance, do you and your friends like to hang out for hours in a restaurant, sipping a soft drink and sharing one plate of french fries? If so, think back to the last time you waited impatiently for a table while someone read every section of the newspaper cover to cover. Dawdling in the diner is fine if it's the middle of the afternoon and no one is waiting for a table. But if there's a line, finish up quickly and continue your conversation somewhere else. Both the people who want to sit down and eat and the owners of the restaurant will appreciate your thoughtfulness.

In a restaurant where you're waited on, always leave a tip even if you didn't order much food. Waiters and waitresses usually earn small salaries, and they depend on tip money. The longer you take up a table, the bigger your tip should be, because you've deprived your server of another customer at that table.

Perhaps you're wondering how much tip you're supposed to leave. You're not alone; plenty of adults wonder the same thing, and they've had much more practice. A tip of 15 percent of the bill has been the standard amount for many years; for extra service, some people leave 20 percent.

Here's an easy way to figure out 15 percent of a total. Drop the last digit of the total and you'll have 10 percent; take half that amount (5 percent) and add it to the 10-percent number. Example: the bill is $12.95;

drop the 5; $1.29 is 10 percent. Round up to $1.30 to make things easier. Half of $1.30 is $.65; add that to the 10 percent, and you get $1.95, which is 15 percent of the bill. So leave two dollars as a tip. Of course, if you've been sitting there for an hour and a half getting refills of your ice water, add another fifty cents; this brings your tip to just under 20 percent.

In a fast-food restaurant or a food court at a mall, you don't have to leave a tip, because there are no waiters or waitresses to leave it for. You get to be your own waiter at these places. When you're ready to leave, pick up your trash and put it in the garbage bin (their large size and prominent signs make them easy to spot). You probably appreciate finding a clean table when you go to a fast-food place, so you can understand how happy you'll make the next hungry person when you clean up your mess. You do the same thing in the school cafeteria, don't you?

Are there other steps you can take to change the way adults view kids in general and you in particular? Of course there are! The next time you see an elderly man who's having trouble getting a grocery item from the bottom shelf, you could bend down and get it for him. Use your youth and physical abilities to advantage. That very pregnant woman loaded down with packages will probably appreciate it when you offer her your seat on the bus. And so will the other passengers who see you doing your good deed for the day.

But try not to feel hurt if something you consider

an act of kindness isn't taken the way you'd thought it would be.

Dear K.T.:

I read your column faithfully and I usually think you've got good advice. But the other day I tried to apply your "golden rule" idea, and it didn't work out very well.

I was on the bus and this old man got on. He looked kind of disgusting because he had spilled food on his tie and shirt and his jacket was sort of rumpled. Then he had trouble finding the right change and a bunch of people behind him were muttering about him taking so much time when they were trying to get on.

The bus was full and I felt sorry for him, so when he got to where I was sitting, I offered him my seat. He not only refused to take it, but he was pretty rude about it, too. I could feel the other people on the bus looking at me the whole rest of the way. I was so embarrassed—I just wanted to crawl into a hole and pull it in after me.

From now on I'm

No More Ms. Nice Guy

Dear No More:

I can see why you were upset—no one deserves to have her kind offer refused rudely.

But my guess is that people were staring at you and the old man because they couldn't believe he was so ungrateful.

I can't excuse the man's rudeness, but I can see some possible explanations for his behavior. Some older people are angry at life because they can't do things as easily or well as they used to. They want to continue living independently, but it gets harder and harder for them to do that.

Maybe this man dresses in a jacket and tie because he wants to feel like the able businessman he once was. And perhaps he knew he'd spilled food down his front and was embarrassed by it. Then, when he fumbled for the correct bus money, he was frustrated because he used to be able to pick out those coins more speedily. By the time he reached you, he might have been feeling helpless and upset with himself, and having a girl offer him a seat was the last straw. After all, he probably was brought up to believe that men give up their seats to women, not the other way around.

Or maybe he was just an old grouch who used to be a young grouch.

No matter what his reasons were, yours are the ones that count. I hope this unfortunate incident won't stop you from trying to help to others in the future. You are obviously a kind and caring person.

A half century ago, men weren't expected only to give women their seats on a bus; women were thought of as needing help and protection, and men were supposed to provide it. Men were taught to hold doors open for women, to let women out of elevators first, and to walk on the outside of the sidewalk to protect women from the mud splashes of passing vehicles. They were also supposed to open the passenger door of a car and help the woman in (naturally, she wasn't doing the driving).

Few men automatically open the car door for a woman anymore. And few women these days expect men to treat them as if they might break. But many people, especially older ones, appreciate the courtesy these gestures represent. Whether you're a boy or a girl, you'll find that adults are amazed and impressed when you hold a door open instead of letting it slam in their faces.

There are bound to be times when you're viewed with suspicion just because you're a kid. It's not fair that you sometimes suffer because of other kids' bad behavior. But just as their actions may cause negative feelings, what you do can create the opposite effect. Your actions send a strong message to the people around you, so let that message be a positive one.

Chapter 9: On Vacation

A FAMILY VACATION is a time for fun, but it may have hidden difficulties as well. During a vacation, you'll be spending almost all your time with your family instead of just the evenings and weekends. You won't have your regular routines and activities to keep you interested and busy. Decisions have to be made as a group, and that involves trying to keep everyone happy. All this unaccustomed togetherness means that every member of the family needs to be especially sensitive to the moods and needs of the others.

One of the biggest problems in a family vacation is that everyone has slightly different expectations, and it's unlikely that all of them will be met. If your family doesn't discuss what each of you hopes for, your vacation can end up being frustrating and unpleasant for everyone. Remember, none of you is a mind reader.

Try asking your family to hold a planning meeting. This doesn't necessarily mean making a plan for each day of the trip; many people find surprise events the best parts of their vacations. But you can all talk over what you'd like to do. If you don't share your thoughts and desires with your family, you have only yourself to blame if things don't turn out the way you wanted them to.

If the vacation will include a lengthy car, bus, train, or plane trip, you need to think ahead. How will you occupy yourself during those long hours? Are you expected to help keep younger brothers and sisters amused while you travel?

Just sitting and looking out a window at the passing scenery can get pretty boring after a while. Taking along a book to read or stationery to write notes to friends is always a good idea. But if your younger brother and sister have nothing to do but watch you read, they're not going to be happy. Maybe there are some games you can play with them. Many card and board games will work fine on almost any mode of transportation. Or what about all those singing and counting games? Probably the other people on the bus or plane wouldn't be thrilled if you and your brother sang a million verses of some song at the top of your lungs! But if it's only your family together in a car, songs are a great way to make the miles go by faster.

Perhaps this unpaid baby-sitting doesn't seem to

have much to do with manners. But bored, cranky kids lead to unhappy, frustrated parents. Whatever you can do to keep younger members of your family entertained on a long trip will be much appreciated by everyone. This kind of consideration for others is the essence of good manners.

Visiting grandparents or other relatives in a different part of the country can be terrific. They're probably thrilled to see you and your family, and you get to explore a new place. But even among people who love each other, friction can arise. It's important to remember that you're staying in someone else's house; although they're family, it's not the same as being at home. For instance, if Grandma and Grandpa don't approve of kids being excused from dinner before everyone is finished eating, you can't leave the table early when you're staying with them. Or, if your grandparents' house is full of fragile bric-a-brac, you'll have to slow down and be extra careful not to break things. Older relatives probably aren't used to having kids around anymore. Cheerfully accepting the rules of the house will make the visit more fun for the whole family, and will make your parents feel proud of you.

Some kids' grandparents are active, vigorous people who never seem to get tired. Others may not have enough energy to keep up with someone your age. Try to adjust your thinking and keep their age and physical limitations in mind. You don't want to embarrass Grandpa by expecting him to stay up until midnight to watch horror movies with you if he's used to being in bed by nine-thirty.

Going on vacation with a parent and a stepparent can be a little awkward. Even if you don't end up sharing one bedroom, you—or your stepparent—may feel a bit uncomfortable with so much togetherness. Making an effort to be especially considerate and obliging will smooth the difficult moments. Your stepparent will feel genuinely included, and your mom or dad will appreciate your thoughtfulness.

Maybe your vacation will include a stay at a hotel, resort, or campground. Any kind of public accommodation has rules that guests must follow. Whether it's the policy on kids swimming in the motel pool, or the requirement that everyone rides in groups at a dude ranch, or campfire and trail rules at a campground, there are bound to be some sort of restrictions on your actions. People who run these places have to deal with zillions of strangers with zillions of ways of doing things. They couldn't stay in business without regulations to keep some sense of safety and order. The sooner you find out what the limitations and expectations are, the more fun you'll be able to have. You won't have to worry that someone is going to yell at you over some simple rule you didn't even know existed.

You may think that some of the rules are ridiculous. For example, it's annoying to have to trek back to your room and change because no jeans are allowed in the restaurant for dinner. Even worse, lots of hotels require that you wear a cover-up over your swimsuit when you're in the lobby or the elevators. Still, if this is where your family is spending the vacation, you're better off accepting the dress code gracefully. Making a scene won't change it and will only cause embarrassment and bad feelings.

Besides the actual rules, there is another important thing to keep in mind when staying in public places: consideration of others. Everyone is different. Some people like to get up at the crack of dawn; others are late sleepers. Some people think lots of sound around them is great; others prefer peace and quiet. There are readers and action people and those who are both. No matter what category you belong to, you want to do things the way you prefer; just keep in mind that everyone else feels the same way.

Dear K.T.:

When we were on vacation staying at this hotel, my little brother and I were watching TV and the people in the next room pounded on the wall and yelled at us to keep the noise down. We turned down the TV, but they complained again. The volume was so low we could hardly hear the TV ourselves. What should I have done? After all, why have TVs in hotel rooms if people can't use them?

Puzzled

Dear Puzzled:

This is a problem with no good solution, since there are so many factors that could enter into it.

You say the people next door complained about the noise, not the TV. Is it possible that you and your brother got a fit of the giggles during some comedy show and that's what they were really complaining about? Some sounds carry better than others—I'm sure you've noticed that yourself. High-pitched squeals carry very well indeed.

Also, while some hotels have good sound-proofing, others have paper-thin walls. Next time you stay somewhere, listen to see how much you can hear your neighbors, and judge your actions accordingly. If you can hear their TV, they can hear yours, so start out with the volume low.

By the way, you don't say what time this

happened. If it was early evening, then every-one should expect a little noise. If it was three in the morning, then your neighbors have a right to expect total quiet. And they would be right to wonder what you were doing up so late.

In a public place where you pay for your room, the rules are usually pretty clear. But staying in someone else's house can be sort of tricky. A good rule of thumb is to behave a little better than you do in your own home. No one is going to complain if you are extra helpful!

This kind of vacation can be a lot of fun, especially if there are kids about your age to do things with. And you can usually figure out what the house rules are by seeing how the kids act.

But even if the kids who live in the house run around screaming and yelling all the time and never make their beds or help with the dishes, don't think that's okay behavior for you. (If that's the case, your parents will be praying that you don't pick up these bad habits, and your consideration for the adults in the house will be much appreciated.)

No matter how the other kids act, there are unspo-ken "houseguest rules" that you should follow. Make your bed and keep your stuff orderly. Leave the bath-room neat and tidy. Offer to help with meal chores such as setting the table, clearing it, and doing the dishes. If you have a snack in front of the TV, take your plate, glass, napkin, or whatever back to the kitchen when you're finished, instead of waiting for someone else to clear up after you (you do this in your own home anyway, don't you?). Having extra people in the house puts a strain on the hosts, and your helpfulness will make you and your family more welcome to come back again.

Dear K.T.:

Last weekend we all visited Mr. and Mrs. Strauss, who are friends of my folks. After we left, my mom told me that I should have been more helpful while we were there. She seemed kind of disappointed in me.

I did help, or at least I offered to. But every time I said I'd help, Mrs. Strauss told me not to bother, that she'd rather do it herself. So what's my mom complaining about?

Mystified

Dear Mystified:

There's a big difference between mumbling an offer to help with the dishes as you head for the TV in the living room and actually picking up a couple of plates after dinner and carrying them into the kitchen. The idea is not only to offer to help, but to act as though you mean it.

Some people really don't want guests to assist them. I don't understand this myself, but

I guess they think guests should relax and enjoy themselves. Or maybe they want things done exactly their own way and figure no one else can do it right.

You need to find out from your mom whether she's complaining to you because her friend complained to her, or whether she's upset because you ended up not doing things she thought you should be doing. If her friend complained, then maybe your offers didn't sound very genuine. In that case, your mom has a right to be a little disappointed.

If not, try asking your mom specifically how she'd like you to be more helpful next time. Maybe she'll see that she was being a little hard on you, or maybe you'll get some good tips that will make your next trip end more happily.

If you visit a house where there aren't any children, you have to pay special attention. Even if your parents' friends have children who are now grown, they've probably forgotten what it's like to have kids in the house. They may end up treating you like a two-year-old and at the same time expecting you to act like an adult. Try not to feel insulted when they expect you to go to bed right after dinner, or when they assume you want to sit inside all evening and listen to their conversation with your parents about the people they all knew way back when.

There's not much you can do about these mixed messages. If you're just staying overnight, make the best of things—you can laugh about it later with your parents. If you're staying longer, enlist your parents' support in readjusting the rules.

Vacations by definition are a lot of fun. And by being considerate of both your family and others, you can make yours even better.

Chapter 10: The Meaning of Manners

It's EASY TO SEE that having good manners helps you get along with the other people in your life—with your family, your friends, your classmates and teachers, even total strangers. Since it's unlikely that you live alone on a desert island, getting along with others is pretty important. And have you noticed that people who are rude and obnoxious usually don't seem to be very happy?

The social skills that most people mean when they talk about manners—things like making proper introductions or using the right fork at a dinner party—help to make everyday interactions with others easier. But good manners are more than that. And showing consideration by behaving politely reduces the stress that seems to invade everyone's life.

Imagine that you're rushing to the library to get a reserve book you need, so you can look up some information for the paper that's due tomorrow. The reason you're rushing is that you've just finished taking a make-up test in math, and you're supposed to be at basketball practice in five minutes.

Scenario 1: You get to the librarian's desk, only to see Bob Burns walking away with the only copy of the book you need—he's just checked it out. When you tell him you really need the book just for tonight, he shrugs his shoulders and says, "Too bad. You shoulda got here sooner. I'll be using this book for the next two weeks for my background research." The librarian helps you find another book; it's not exactly what you need, but it's the best you can hope for now. As you go toward the library door, Wendy Walker pushes it open and leaves ahead of you; she glances back and sees you but doesn't bother to hold the door open. Instead, she lets it slam back just as you reach it, and your pile of books goes flying. Frantically, you pick them all up and race to the gym, but you're late for practice. Getting a book at the library is a valid excuse, but Jan Jones, your best friend on the team, forgot to tell the coach that's where you were, so you have to do ten laps around the gym as punishment. You're angry and upset, and when practice starts, you can't concentrate on what you're doing, so the coach yells at you.

A terrible afternoon, right? Now look at Scenario 2:

When you explain your problem to Bob Burns, he says he'll be happy to let you use the book this evening, as long as you give it to him tomorrow morning. You thank him profusely, thinking what a nice guy he is. As you leave, Wendy Walker sees you balancing all your books and holds the door open for you, making a joke about how you need a supermarket cart to carry your stuff. Laughing, you thank her, too. When you get to the gym, the coach asks if you finished what you needed to do at the library. You smile gratefully at Jan, who obviously remembered to explain where you were. The coach takes the opportunity to remind the whole team that schoolwork comes before sports practice. When practice starts, you're feeling relaxed and confident and you're able to pay attention to the plays you're learning today.

Everybody in Scenario 2 feels great. Bob and Wendy know they've been helpful to you, and your thanks showed each of them how much you appreciated their behavior. Jan feels good about helping you out by remembering to pass on your message to the coach, while the coach feels good about encouraging you and other players to take your schoolwork seriously. You, of course, feel terrific. Because everyone was so considerate, everything worked out perfectly.

Did Bob, Wendy, Jan, and the coach have good manners in this scenario, or were they just being nice? Have you considered that "just being nice" is the foun-

102

dation of politeness? Being kind and helpful is what good manners is all about. Maybe you've met people who do everything "correctly" in an icy-cold, scornful way; they are guilty of bad manners, because they clearly don't care about the feelings of others.

You might say that the seed from which any system of good manners grows is the golden rule: Treat other people the way you'd like them to treat you. For centuries, many people have considered this rule the most important guiding principle of human society. We all want others to treat us fairly, honestly, and kindly. If we act that way ourselves, others are likely to act the same way toward us.

ELIZABETH JAMES and **CAROL BARKIN** have coauthored more than thirty books for children and young adults. Their successful how-to books include *How to Write Your Best Book Report, How to Write a Great School Report, How to Write a Term Paper,* and *Sincerely Yours: How to Write Great Letters.* The two also write suspense novels for young adults under the joint pseudonym Beverly Hastings. Their most recent book for Clarion was *The New Complete Babysitter's Handbook,* which ALA *Booklist* called "serious, practical, and chockablock with good advice."

Elizabeth James graduated from Colorado College with a B.A. in mathematics. She lives in Beverly Hills, California.

Carol Barkin received a B.A. in English from Radcliffe College. She lives in Hastings-on-Hudson, New York.

Both Elizabeth James and Carol Barkin have very good manners.